Homelight

ALSO BY LOLA HASKINS

Asylum: Improvisations on John Clare
How Small, Confronting Morning
The Grace to Leave
Fifteen Florida Cemeteries: Strange Tales Unearthed
Still, the Mountain
Not Feathers Yet: A Beginner's Guide to the Poetic Life
Solutions Beginning with A
Desire Lines: New and Selected Poems
The Rim Benders
Extranjera
A Lifetime from Any Land We Knew
Visions of Florida
Hunger
Forty-Four Ambitions for the Piano.
Castings
Across Her Broad Lap Something Wonderful
Planting the Children

Homelight

Lola Haskins

Charlotte Center for Literary Arts, Inc.
Charlotte, North Carolina
charlottelit.org

ISBN: 978-1-960558-03-9

Library of Congress Control Number: 2023942320

Cover and author photos by Charles Brown

Charlotte Lit Press
Charlotte Center for Literary Arts, Inc.
PO Box 18607, Charlotte, NC 28218
charlottelit.org/press

PROUD MEMBER

[clmp]

COMMUNITY OF LITERARY MAGAZINES & PRESSES
W W W . C L M P . O R G

Contents

7 Rehearsing

1
On the Shoulders of Giants

Part One

Why Anaïs Nin Would Lie with Me

More than the shells on the beach
I desire
the shells in the mountains.

The shells on the beach break
easily.
The shells in the mountains

are ancient seas, turned bone.
I wake,
craving them with my tongue.

~ after Sappho

Daybreak

A sculptor has carved bare thighs
along the ridge.

In a dark recess,

mosses bloom. The light slides
up, over the rocks

the light slides down.

         ~ after Ho Xuan Huong

Song

The mountains shake
   the mountains fall.
     The sea rises
   the sea turns dust.
  In spring when the peach trees
     flower   I will fly from here
   and if I return not even you
who loved my red sleeves
  the most will know me
    for in such a swoop
who can tell one swallow
from another?

          ~ after Qi Xiaoyao

Mercy, Pity, Peace, and Love

The earth is a kind chair. When I have stopped breathing, she will not tell me I must get up.

Above, a nest; below, torn feathers connected by a shred of flesh.

The baby, full, falls asleep at his mother's nipple.

After the rain, frogs appear who were never there before.

Then, as all that surrounds us is miracle, like miracles, they sing.

~ after William Blake and John Clare

At Sixty

Whoever has not licked money will never know the intimacy of coins.

Whoever has not laid seeds into the earth will have blank fingernails.

Whoever has not felt tautness in her chest will not recognize the mountain.

Whoever has not put on her second skin will leave it in her closet.

Whoever has not danced the rhumba will not slick a wet curl to her cheek.

Whoever has not spread her thighs will not love that small creek.

Whoever is rushing down the street will not notice the dark red plum leaf falling.

~ after Rainer Maria Rilke

His Poems

Some lie, pins set, in a field of phlox, a living room, the road to the store;
the smallest contact and they explode; hence, the poet's country is full
of the limbless.

Others, read without protection, whiten a watcher's eyes instantly so
he spends the rest of his life in snow.

The poet's readers understand the risks, yet each book he flings
into the crowd lands in a pair of eager hands.

How can this be? Is it a trick the poet plays? Who are these readers?
What can we do to bring them here?

~ after Zbigiew Herbert

The Watcher

Fourteen red-crowned cranes graze on the edge
of the wetland. I hold my breath and spread my roots.
One after another lifts off and disappears over
the far trees. I raise my arms to celebrate the air
that has them now. Lost in my own priesthood,
it takes me longer than it should to notice that
four cranes have stayed behind. They dip into
the sunlit dark-blue water, swallow, dip again.
I wait. They stay. Who am I to understand any of this?

~ after Mary Oliver

Dear William

The minute I met the boy
you were I knew I'd run
away with him   if only
he'd ask   Ever since

I was small I've been
finding houses too and
like you my father said
I'd made them up
I wish I could have told

you sooner but here are
the ones I remember best
The little clapboard house
in the woods where
an old couple'd lived
all their married lives

It had lace curtains she
must have hung and
two rocking chairs on
the white porch he'd
tended so lovingly
it glowed   I was ten
The other I found later

A rusty-tin-roofed shack
a battered broom leaning
beside its door and inside
empty except for some
animal scat and a card
table in the front room

holding a plate heaped
with desiccated bones
and   oh yes a single
chair knocked over as if
the person sitting on it

had had to move fast
Which William you did
I'm your sister I'd have
said   thinking *Touch me*

    ~ after W. S. Merwin

Part Two

Conserving Michelangelo

The drawing is pale brown ink over cream paper. A diagonal tear crosses from the arches on the left to the robe of the figure on the right, then disappears—as if a bird had suddenly flown through Michelangelo's studio and he, taking its path for a sign, had put it in. The whole is twice-mounted, first simply by Michelangelo's great-nephew, then, a century, later, in grander style—but both mounts, being too small, have left the paper rippled.

Marjorie leans over her work, one palm flat on its either side, as if she were shielding it with her body. Which she, passionately, is. She wants it never to become a sadness, like that of a woman on whom it slowly dawns that by destroying her wrinkles, she has lost her greatest beauty: the time she wears on her face.

Having thought this, Marjorie decides she was right about the sadness, but that a drawing's life is more complicated than a woman's. Before she can know what to mend and what to leave alone, she must see it free. She tests glues, settles on seaweed gel then treats the mounts two inches at a time, flattening each gel worm with her hand. When she finishes the trip, since like Machaut her end is her beginning, she picks up a damp brush. In this work she is a painter, and a poet too—and patiently, for painters and poets need patience in moments as delicate as these, she gentles the glue away.

Now, with the drawing naked on the table before her, she can see that the linen and flax paper on which it's rendered—the strongest the world has ever known—has, after a lifetime of too much light, become tearable and worse, warped. Because this cannot stand, she cradles it, lays it carefully into a plastic box, covers the lid with weights so that not one of its inspirations can escape—and leaves it there. Hours later, she returns, takes it out, presses it between blotters, lays it back. Leaves it, takes it out, presses it, lays it back. What are weeks compared to centuries? What is her own life, compared to the beauty of these pale lines, this washed paper, the calm of the monk it shelters? Compared to the brilliance of the hand that made the monk?

When she has done all she can, the drawing lies nearly flat. But not quite. It's not the matting now, but the tear, carelessly-mended so long ago, that disturbs its surface. But then it comes to her: the tear is history, is a testament to human fallibility, even Michelangelo's since it must have happened in his studio.

An Incident in Michelangelo's Studio. What could be more alive, she thinks, than that: the tear, the wrinkles, the truth. Oh, how she adores every moment she spends with her eyes, her hands, her heart, in the presence of genius; how lucky she is that the heavens have allowed her to dance this way, how unlike herself but poetic nevertheless, are the slow surgeries of her life.

For Marjorie Shelley
Curator of Works on Paper
Metropolitan Museum of Art

2
Wings

Because We Fail to Look Up

we miss the black circlers
in the bare sky
the blue and yellow parula
in the woods
the osprey
over the river

miss the wispy clouds
that will not return
the stars that every night
are closer to gone.

Most of us live
and die
as if the earth
under our feet
were all there is

but we should
not blame ourselves
for in the end
who is not afraid.

Seeing God

Perched on a stone that could be a mountain, he does not move.
The sun polishes his russet breast, his small head, his obsidian eyes
and hooked beak.   It bronzes the claws that quiet the struggling creatures
he lifts towards the angels, whose hands are trembling with hunger.

The Cranes

Early this morning,
I biked to a field I know
to watch them touch
down, and one by one

lower their heads to the
grass. And it brought back
something that happened
when I was very young.

My mother had left me
alone in the sun-wet
plaza when suddenly
on the steps a tall priest

appeared. I can still see
his spread gray wings
and hear his call, made
not of words but of

clatter and trill, which
was why, when he turned
away and began to stalk
the stones, up towards

the darkened bell, I had
to follow. Some dreams
were never dreams at all.
I know that now.

Goldfinch

If I had a yellow breast, I would perch in high shadows.
And in my dreams, if I had to fly, I would fly quickly

because if I shone, the tabby on the ground would
not be fooled. He knows these trees do not flower.

Above me, bark rains down. And as his lifting paw
reaches me I sense *Don't move.* And I don't.

At the Park

The oaks overhead tremble with robins
who flit and land, flit and land, as if
there's so much to see they can't stop
looking. Though I'm drab as dead leaves
from above, when I rise and my sisters rise,
we call to each other like children swinging
lanterns, stars among the darkened trees.

The Racing Pigeon

Once I was let hold
a two-day old chick,
warm and pulsing
in my hand, and as

I stroked its beak,
I came to wonder
about home, and
whether if I were

abandoned between
deep-set hills that
would neither kill me
nor make me happy,

I would give up
everything
I had
to fly there.

The Dove

Today I saw a soft gray dove, as elegant
as the most elegant Frenchwoman, perched
on a fence rail as if all Paris were spread
before her who as I went by, neither flew

nor called. And what passed between us
I understood: I was not worth her throat.
And nothing—not mist nor thicketry
nor windy leaves not even the darkest

depths of night can conceal her now.
I would know that silence anywhere.

Swallowtail Kite

You are a split-tailed ship, sailing the sky as if the trees below were
nothing. You live hatch to death without ever touching the ground.

Because I was born of earth as plants are born, I know that though
we say airplanes "fly," it's clear that they, having no will, cannot.

Still, Majesty, don't underestimate the trees since of all living creatures
only they can both hold their ground and reach for your wings at once.

Comparisons can be so pretty. When I asked my granddaughter
why she was so sure Roy Rogers was better than the Lone Ranger

she said because Roy can lean all the way to the ground off Trigger
and pick something up but the Lone Ranger could *never* do that.

The Woodpecker

He swoops,
dips as if
he has forgotten
something,
and swoops again.

Eventually, he lands
over my head
so high up
I almost fall over
backwards

watching him
hammer at the tree
like a resolute
toddler
pounding pegs.

Oh Woodpecker
Woodpecker
Woodpecker,
I like your hat!

Ask an Ornithologist

Ibises

Q. Do two double ibises wading in the shallows make a quartet?

A. No, because only the top ones are ibises. The bottom, upside-down ones are known as "water birds."

Goldfinches

Q. Is there any particular word for a flock of goldfinches?

A. Yes, there is. The collective term for goldfinches is "mint" unless you encounter the birds after sunset, in which case it is "after-dinner mint."

Robins

Q. Why do robins sing so loudly?

A. They're all deaf.

Chickens

Q. What does it mean when a hen goes BAWK bawk bawk BAWK (repeated) bawk bawk bawk bawwwwk?

A. It means that she has just laid an egg and is celebrating.

Q. Will she celebrate again when it hatches?

A. No.

Birds on Wires

Q.   Why do birds sit on power lines even in places where there are plenty of trees?

A.   Most of what you're seeing is listening devices. The few actual birds there belong to species that happen to be attracted to silhouettes, and any individuals who show signs of being onto the devices are instantly taken out (you must have read about birds being electrocuted on wires). And now you're "in the know," isn't it clear why the "birds-on-wire" density is greatest in heavily-populated places?*

Note to the reader: My name isn't really "An Ornithologist" — it's Rupert Q. Mills — but I decided on anonymity when I started my column so I could answer questions like this without running afowl of the NSA, the KGB, whatever.

*Because more people means more conversations to listen to. Obviously.

3
And They Are Gone

Dominion

We name the birds and think those are their names

    but our throats are helpless when calling flights pass over

    and we can't taste the earth that comes up with the worm in a robin's beak

    nor in the worst moments of our lives can we approach the way an owl sobs.

We analyze the sky using charts   one phenomenon at a time

    yet when light pierces the clouds like our visions of God we turn into

    open mouths and when that light enters us   no matter how much

    we want to keep it   because we do not have the tools we can never.

We wade through undergrowth whose leaves and sticks are our words for them

    but the nodules and stitchings on our ankles will always know more about plants

    than we do and we have no idea what to call the way trees dwarf us nor when

    we hold them how to interpret the patterns their barks leave on our cheeks.

We have stories but we cannot parse them so when we step on a seedling struggling

    through a crack we never think of Cain and Abel   nor does the way water

    cascades towards us from high and ancient rock bring Rapunzel to mind

    nor when we look at the stars do we remember *As it was in the beginning.*

When will we understand that all our classifications are only attempted dust?

    That nothing pinned to a card is true? That sight and hearing

    and taste and our hearts and our brains and the tips of our fingers

    are like yellow butterflies? Reach for them and they are gone.

Seeds: A Sequence

Prologue

*Fire, air, earth, water, and space—if you don't want the seed,
you can't have those either.* ~Kabir

From the cones bursting like grenades
        over rivers of deer and snakes
        and small animals desperate
    to elude the terrible heat   bright shoots

appear   and before we can blink
        they're spreading over the burnt ground
        like a tide   And the spires of the sequoias
        they will become will thrust upwards
    for thousands of what we   who think
  we can reckon time   call years

Inside our bodies is a seed and inside
        the seed is our body again, and on and on
        until the day we decide our hall of mirrors
    is everything that matters in the world
  and in that moment   all we are will end

but the stars whose seeds we were will
    still shine   over a land whose creatures
        resemble nothing we've ever seen
  and whose souls we cannot imagine

And the plants of this new land
        large or small   will lift their umbrellas
        over their kin and over those who
        are not their kin   And on certain nights
        the stars will descend from the sky
    to float on the sea which   no longer
  in thrall to our slightest whim
will by the tall moon's grace   be holy again

The Skein of the Sea

winds blue and turquoise and green and gray
                  and curls back on itself
                           And all the sands
belong to it   and all the mountains
                  and lost cities whose sky is water
and all the tired swimmers
                it rocked and held
          And all of us who were born breathing
                through our cheeks   belong to it
                no matter that we
have forgotten how gingerly we left it
              balancing on our fins
 And if we were to hang it like a tapestry
            it would flood our houses with
                 its flickering light
the way every night the moon pulls us
          to the dark water on which it floats
over which in dreams
      we like sea birds are always flying
And some day it will wrap itself
    around our bodies   until
like all creatures that struggle
  we fall silent   and
     as our eyes dim
 we will begin to understand
     there has never been
         anything as beautiful as this moment
in which the watery mote we were
   widens
     and becomes everything

The Hundred and One Names of the Wind

We hear them chanted over the domes
              and crosses and glass towers
      of our darkened city
        This has been so since
             there were only tents here
      and first light glittered on rolling sands

And men and women speak them together
           while their children sleep
      who will be taught them when it is time
        the boys with their black curls
           and their sisters alike

For the wind is all around us   For its voices
          have taught us song
      and its swayings   dance   For when we are born
        it gives us breath and when
          like a great love it leaves us
      it takes that breath away

And some of its moods we fear for any day
          of the world it may crush us under
      our houses   and our neighbors too
        But others we prize   for in its pleasure

times, it will skip with us like a cousin
         or stroke our cheeks as tenderly
    as any mother

Still other moods, we cannot fathom   Those
     are the ones that like sudden dogs
       we don't notice until they're upon us
    and not even afterwards
       be we wise or foolish do we
    understand what we have done

Prairie

I tell you there is an ocean
          that is not called ocean
                whose waves ripple from
          one horizon to the other
   under a sky so wide you can walk
     all day under a single cloud
          or walk all day under clouds
     that never pause whose shadows
change the colors of the grasses
          so quickly that they shift
     in a blink   the way the sea
   can shift   or your life   in
   such a way that if   when you
          get home   your son were to ask
          what was it like walking out there
     then add *I mean when you were my age*
you wouldn't know what to say
       And though the old people who
          remember wading waist deep
     in that swaying water when
they were children   would deny it
          some evenings as they look
          out from their porches across
   an expanse so vast that houses are
          marked not by street but by
          section number they
are sometimes moved to kneel
not before God   but before
          this land   which is sea
and earth and clouds and
          the now vanishing sun at once
          and as they bow their heads
     the grasses in their hearts
   whisper until their lives spread
     as far as their closed eyes
          can see and they do not move
     until the silence tells them
that every horizon is filled with stars.

35

Fire: Two Translations

1

Once there was a pine   high on a ridge
    where there were no people   One night
  a hand jagged down from a cloud
    and slashed this pine's bark so that when
        the beetles found it it would die slowly
  feeling its own dust circling its trunk

  Now   lightning as a lover does like it slow
    but it also likes it fast   so as it pulled
      back the hand dropped a spark
       which for weeks lay on its needled bed
    so subtly that if you walked over it
    your foot would not feel warm

But all the while the spark   being lightning's
    child was trying   harder every day
  to make herself beautiful to the wind
  so he would come and breathe on her
    until the two of them became one heat
  free to devour every bush and
    tree and bird and frightened thing
  until they died
      Better to perish in an inferno
      they told each other than
  to close your eyes and call it peace

2

One afternoon Désirée climbed the rickety stairs
    of the barracks to the third floor
      undressed behind the curtain in the corner
    piled her clothes on a chair then emerged
  and perched on the windowsill

her white arms and legs   her hair
a cloud around her face   because Luc
    wanted her where she could be seen
from the street   then   at his beck
    tilted her head a little down

towards the crowds hurrying to
        restaurants and cafes   Luc stood
    by his easel measuring her with
    his hands   She felt them like dry snakes
        sliding along her skin
When he had her his brush began to travel
    up and down   first slowly   then fast
        urgent as an arsonist's torch   shoulders
    neck   waist   thighs   delta   her eyes

all the while fixed on his   He paused
    to think   heedless of the paint
            dripping to his palette

then slashed his brush across her belly
        like a car careening into
            traffic

On break Désirée smoked   tipping her ashes out
    the window Afterwards, she resumed her position
        perfectly Luc thought   as he studied her breasts.

At the end of the day he turned the wet painting
    around for her   She stood beside him
        Her short silk robe brushed his bare leg
    Then there was no robe

4
(In)humanity

Those Who Look Alike but Are Not

Palm stems vee into their fronds like swords.

Palmetto stems are squarely attached.

How many battles have rung out between

men wielding sharp and blunt instruments?

From time to time, the palms and palmettos

philosophize about this. And after all, why not?

They are not the ones destroying the world.

The Coup

I offered them my chest
and told them, go ahead
But even González,
who hated me the most,

could not. How sweetly
habit grows, like mold
on shoes in our hot country.
I told them their own troops,

a prickle of boys, brown hands
slippery on their guns,
were loyal to me and
now I tell them sing,

mouths full of dirt or no.
And even the ones whose
throats I slit, sing.

            ~ Panamá, 1989

Bear

If he is far away, say, shuffling down an embankment, turn around and leave slowly.

If he sees you and starts to approach, stand tall and speak in a low voice.

If a bear charges, running will get you killed. Perhaps he is bluffing.

If a group of bears attacks your village, lie still.

If they are not fooled, fight back with everything they are trying to rip out.

If this means you have to set fire to your country, do it.

~ Ukraine

Freedom of Speech

Jimmy went down the taxi ranks
smashing up Paki cabs.
It was a lark, he was drunk.
He's only one of the lads.

~ North Yorkshire, United Kingdom

Touring the Lower Oklawaha, 2015

The sergeant left the tent saying,
As you were, soldiers.

You enlisted at seventeen to get away from the mill,
having no idea there was a war on. Your platoon was
dropped into Laos to ruck back to Vietnam, with orders
to kill everyone in every village along the way. When I ask
the obvious, you say yes, them too. You lift your T-shirt
to show me the gun you're never without, tucked into
the waistband of your shorts. The river here runs crystal
but above the dam, the fish swim ever more slowly, until
the inevitable haze coats them, turns them on their sides,
and floats them upwards.

~ Vietnam and Florida, USA

Untitled

When every dog we've met is kept inside
or behind a fence
or in a cage
or on the street at the end of a chain
it's not surprising that if we see one free
we fear it.

~ Anywhere, USA

To Three Frozen Scribbles

Para los que murieron de esperanza.

You must have crawled

out of the earth

onto my porch last night

hoping for refuge

and as you died of the cold—

the way Silvestro

when he suddenly knows

he will never reach Gila Bend

drops his dry canteen—

you left me this message.

~ Florida and Arizona, USA

Aleppo

The father speaks of his six month old boy, born here,
who has never seen the sky. The baby, he thinks,
believes the rusty stains on the ceiling of the family's
one room are all there is. The cease fire is temporary.
There is rubble. But today the father showed his son
what he could not have known to dream: air blue as
sapphires, crossed by clouds. The father cannot
remember when he last felt such joy. The people of
Aleppo are on strike against the aid trucks. They do
not want food or clothes, they say. Bring them peace.

~ Syria

5
Corona
2019–2021

Three Panku

Elon

is happy to advertise
that *her* mask
has penises on it.

Bet He Is

Governor DeSantis
has added live wrestling to
his list of essential activities.
I'm a huge fan, he said.

Interim Self-Review

So much awful
poetry!
Come *on,* vaccine!

The Trail

Woods

Home and here are
the only places
I'm allowed
now the world is sick.

Trail

Leaves are
etching the bottoms
of my shoes.

Company

A tiny violet moth
has fallen in love
with my socks.

Beside the Path

some brown and white
mushrooms are
discussing the rain.

Cut-throats

Smilaxes
will get to the top
no matter
who they smother.

Thrum

Whenever the sky
dims
crickets chirp like stars.

When like a Daughter

heat walks down the aisle
my cheeks dampen
past anything
I can wipe away.

Trees

Your barks, my tribe.
Your leaves, my light.
My heart, a bird

who can sing
like the thin edge
of the moon,
large
as her soul
small as a molecule,

sing— imagine!—
as if she had wings.

Luxury

a glossy leaf

a full moon wreathed in branches

a crab spider off-center on her web

lavender clusters of wisteria

ivory flutters of lichen

brown-and-gray velvet fans

dangling white glories

a curve of bone —

I turn each to the light

then walk on, because I know

I can't afford anything here

not even a single raindrop

to wear at my throat.

How to Fall Asleep during a Pandemic

I keep a book on my bedside table for
when my mind won't stop. It never fails,
half a page and I'm gone. My friend
who wrote this book should be pleased.
Not everyone can sit by his reader
like a father singing to a fearful child,
and summon the moon for her
and turn her pillow soft as the sea.

100,000 Lives

When I hold you, my hands do not meet
behind.

When I press my cheek against your bark
I am asking you

to mark me. When I lean into you
you rise towards

the light. Grandfather, thank you
for your calm.

I have been so afraid.

A Walk in May

How many moments like this make a life?
~ From: "Prayer for the Everglades"

This morning on the path
ahead of me, I saw
a doe and fawn
standing very still.
They looked at me
with oceans in their eyes,
before they stepped away.

Streetwise

Migration

The receding rain has left
birds and butterflies of damp
on the sidewalk
and down the block
rivers to guide them.

The Old-Fashioned Street

One brick sticks up diagonally
like a protruding tooth.
Beckett is certain
there's treasure under it.

Walking at Night

Darkened houses.
Rectangular glows
where the shades are drawn.
Where they aren't,
most often, scenes
of blueish light flickering
across a back wall

but once I saw
a man lifting a stack of
flowered plates
off a shelf, as gently
as if he had been kneeling
in a garden.

Archer Road, Late

Threading the gauntlet of neon signs
for businesses that closed
months ago, I sense
a waiting forest,
moonlight in its branches.

6
The Slapped Girl

The Slapped Girl

When I was a child
I used to walk up
the fire road behind
my house. When I
noticed a gleam in
the dirt ahead, I'd
pry it up. At home,
I'd clean it and
cradle it in my hand.
Sometimes it
would tremble me,
how safe it seemed.

1962

The moment at the top of the drive
when my first love turned to say again,
Come now, returns with the evening star

as does the rush of white air that
partnered him when he jumped,
then exploded every bit of him,

khaki shirt and all, when he hit
the bay. Who but a fool believes
that a poem may be got for nothing?

Back

1

In 1968
   when we set out for Brazil on a motor scooter
we didn't care that there were no
                  roads to Brazil
from where we were. When we
   stopped somewhere
     we'd stay a few days then move on,
leaving a suitcase with someone we'd met
   saying, would you keep this for us?
     We'll be right back
  back
       back
  back
 back
   like something twisting and turning
  through the air
until it breaks
   and spills the clothes of our youth
         all over the ground

2

In Phoenix we slept in a room
     so hot it dried the skin
on our bones. In San Juan
we played chess for hours on the porch
  of our boarding house with

Dr. Lavandero
    whose children in Haiti sent him carefully
small money
    because the voodoo priests
  had taken his mind and everything he owned
and he was always
        trying to get back

3

In the seedy clubs we played
        we'd announce that some song
we felt like singing
  was going out by request
and watch the slurry-eyed drunks
  squint through the smoke
    trying to figure out
who asked for *that*

4

Because you could never hold a tune
    I sang all our harmonies
until thirty-five years later
when I left you your backup girl
  and set out alone
            but this time
through the air
  so it doesn't matter
there aren't roads between me
        and where I'm going

yet sometimes when a wing
dips or a wind-wave crests
      and drops
  an overhead spills its contents
and I'm sudden and headlong again
    and falling

The Skunk

The skunk was my birthday present fifteen years before I left G. When we went to pick him up, the first thing he did was reach out from his owner's arms and bite my finger hard enough to draw blood. I should have known then. But I didn't, because once you get the idea something's what you want, it doesn't matter. If W, the new man, leaves you sitting in a restaurant because he just remembered he needed to do the laundry, you'll wait. You'll memorize the menu. You'll stay while everyone's clearing out, you'll stay until they turn off the lights. The skunk was supposed to be de-scented. W was supposed to be on meds too. We used to kiss ourselves dizzy. We never got where we were going. By the end, he might as well have been stray, he might as well have been living under the house.

Four and a Half Years

Maybe when something stops, something lost in us can be heard.
                               ~ Jack Gilbert

1

Maybe when you and your angers are gone,
I'll remember how, when I was twelve,
l leaned against the wall in my best dress
and short white gloves as the other girls
were turned and spun, and it came to me
that the world could end before anyone
asked me to dance. And maybe too,
I'll remember knowing that the couples
waltzing across the windows that faced
the dark, and the reflections of the girl
who watched, were something for each
of us to keep, but why they mattered
I see only now, years after our parents
in their waiting cars, picked us up.

2

Maybe the paintings you demanded back
went home with small changes you won't
have noticed because you thought them
finished when you laid your brushes down.
But, like children who've spent the night
away, maybe your re-hung mountains
and swaying palms are more subtle now,
flecked as they are with dust that isn't
yours. And maybe one morning as you
inspect the lake outside your window,

a speck of that dust will lodge in your eye
and blur the pictures in their frames so
you don't quite know them, any more than
you know who you were when you lived
by those hills, those waters, those shores.

Redemption

When the sky turns blue I'm drawn to look beyond it but every time I try, the fog rolls in off the Golden Gate again. And my first love jumps again and is scattered on the gray waves again like the flowers people throw from boats. And I walk the fire road again to where the dark pines open to hills smeared with red. And I take the turn up at the fork as I always have, because I know the other way leads to where I don't belong.

When the fog rolls away, everything that used to be there is gone. No house on Vallejo Street, no back door whose chain rattled every night at three after the caller I never saw had hung up. No police dog, baring his teeth in the yard. But the story isn't over because what's left is no protection against last year's man who said he loved me then night after night idled his car in my driveway in the dark then knocked my mailbox off its post—it fell like a punched child—and finally broke into my garage and took what he'd wanted all along—not my bicycle but boxes and boxes of my self. I can still see my faces on the backs of those books, burning. He must have enjoyed watching each tiny image curl and turn to ash. He must have warmed his hands over the fire.

The Secret Life

Todos tenemos tres vidas: la privada, la pública, y la secreta.
~ Gabriel Garcia Marquez

Dreaming of You

We're walking hand in hand through a forest carpeted with bluebells. The sun is trembling in the leaves the way my hand trembled when I first realized I loved you.

*

It's midnight. We're lying on a bed next to the sea, on which, kiss after kiss, the waves are breaking.

*

When you pause in the middle of a block, and I see my face in your brown eyes, I suddenly realize that I could die of this.

*

On a hill, under millions of stars stands a house, dark except for a candle shining softly in an upstairs window. When we see the candle, we know that this is our home, that it has always been our home.

La Dichosa

I call you under my breath and
when you hear your name

my phone shines in the dark.
You are the path

of the moon on the water.
You are the star

by which I steer
Angel, Ángel, Amor.

Nuestro Amor

The bottom of the Marianna Trench
seven miles down,
deeper than that.

Like the shimmery dew that clings
to the morning grass,
but more lasting.

The solitaire's song in the ferns
of a cloud forest,
sweeter than that.

Like the pin-fluff of her fledgling,
new to the air
but more delicate.

The night sky on the top
of Annapurna
starrier than that.

La Luna

One night, at exactly
the same moment,
you and I walk out
of our separate houses.
And when we see

the full moon,
gold and shining,
tears stream down
each of our faces
because we have just
realized we no longer
want anything we used
to crave. Not even her.

Proyección: Después de la Pelea

When the wind dies and all is hot and still
we will pick yellow petals and throw them
in the water and see how, even so, they float.

Though We Can Never Be Together

I live with you
in the interstice between breath and breath
in the cool damp hollows tides leave in the sand
and when the sky turns heal-all blue
I fly beside you

and faithfully
every morning we send each other circling hearts
and every bedtime, kisses.
And I wear you
the way a Sikh wears his cord
under his clothes
in token of the ineffable beauty of the world.

7
Rehearsing

The Salt Marsh

At dusk the water turns melted pearl
and the grasses glow like the lights of houses
or as if they have just fallen in love,
both the new greens and last season's
browns, tipped with cinnamon.

My kayak slides easily into
the water I part with each stroke
and behind me a silver wake
forms, then vanishes
as if it and I had never been.

Watermelon Pond

One spring day you and I are
walking a path of sand mixed
with mud beside a lotus-dotted
plain of water that stretches
as far as we can see, but not
until I turn to you to comment
on how beautiful all this is
do I realize you're not there.
Almost to the horizon, a heron
is perching on a branch that
juts out of the lake. How strange,
that in all our years of friendship,
I never once noticed your wings.

       ~ for CS, 1935–2019

The Delivery

~ Each raindrop vanishes into all the drops before it.

Last night Mel

watched the lake

turn slowly rose

then gold, then

dark, like a cloak

slipped over

his shoulders

by a kind god.

And then he died,

not in pain

and not hungry.

~ for MR, 1932–2014

Rehearsing

When you were little,
I'd lullaby you every night,
stroking your back
lighter and lighter
until I was feathers

until I didn't exist.

        ~ for SW, 1970–

The Discovery

On walking, in my seventies, down a leafy street
behind two women in their early forties who
are chatting to each other as companionably
as birds on a limb, and having thought, with
happy anticipation, ah, I'll be their age soon!
it occurs to me that I've lost my mind—but
just then the clouds evanesce and light pours
through the oaks and ash, to form lace on
the pavement lovely enough to be sewn
into dresses, and I see that time is as
random as the patterns the sun makes on
any given day as it filters through leaves,
and as illusory as a baby being born, and
as strange as the years of our lives that
go by without returning, and as equal as
the one friend's auburn hair and the red leaf
she steps over, which the wind has abandoned
for love of her. And now, having finally
seen that the world is every minute new,
I realize that I'm only a little younger than
those women after all, and I step between
them, and we speak as we walk, and by
the time we part, each of us in her own way
has told the others how lucky she is,
to have been alive in such a beautiful place.

Acknowledgments

Some of the poems in this book have previously appeared in the following magazines:

American Journal of Poetry: "Walking at Night"
Cadence: "Goldfinch"
Cave Wall: "The Cranes"
Crab Creek Review: "Aleppo"
Gargoyle: "100,000 Lives," "Watermelon Pond," "Rehearsal," "Because we Refuse to Look Up" and "Four Panku"
Georgia Review: "Seeing God" and "The Watcher"
I-70 Review: "Ask an Ornithologist"
New Letters: "The Skunk" and "How to Fall Asleep During a Pandemic,"
The New York Quarterly: "The Slapped Girl"
On the Seawall: "Dominion," "Conserving Michelangelo" and "Four and a Half Years"
Porter Gulch Review: "The Salt Marsh"
Rattle: "The Discovery" and "Touring the Lower Oklawaha"
Salt: "Seeds: A Sequence"
Sandhill Review: "The Trail" and "Luxury"
Seven: "At Sixty"
Terrain: "The Racing Pigeon"
Thorny Locust: "Archer Road, Late"
South Florida Poetry Journal: "Those Who Look Alike but are Not," "The Coup," "Frozen Scribbles," "Redemption" and "1962"

"100,000 Lives" which originally appeared in *Gargoyle,* was reprinted in *Cooch Nehar Magazine* (India).

"The Coup" placed in the Simon Daro Davidowitz International Poetry Competition. Carolyn Forche was the judge.

About the Author

Besides 13 books of poetry, Lola Haskins has published three of prose, including *Fifteen Florida Cemeteries: Strange Tales Unearthed* (University Press of Florida), *Not Feathers Yet: A Beginner's Guide to the Poetic Life* (University of Nebraska Press), and *Solutions Beginning with A* (Modernbook), a collection of fables about women illustrated by Maggie Taylor.

The past ten or fifteen years have seen ventures into the natural world, both in poetry and prose. Her poem "Prayer for the Everglades" ends the otherwise prose *The Book of the Everglades* (Milkweed), and another poem, "The View from Cedar Key," is one of two poems in *UnspOILed (Heart of the Earth)*, a book of citizens' responses to the Gulf, given to all state legislators prior to the Deepwater Horizon oil spill. *How Small, Confronting Morning* (Jacar) is set in the woods and on the waters of north-central Florida. She has also written an as-yet unpublished collection of personal essays beginning in Florida state parks, called *Wind, the Grass, and Us.*

Haskins particularly relishes collaboration, especially with musicians. She and cellist Ben Noyes created a CD of poems from *The Grace to Leave.* Composer Paul Richards (University of Florida Department of Music) has issued a two CD set of all forty-four of her ambitions for the piano for voice and piano. Composer Willis Bodine's settings for choir and hand bells of 11 of her nature poems concluded University of Floridas 2012 Choral Music Festival. She has also collaborated on a number of occasions with visual artists, most recently with collagist Derek Gores; and with dancers, most recently with choreographer Judy Skinner of Dance Alive! in "Land of La Chua," which premiered at UF's Performing Arts Center in Spring 2019. Two favorite past ventures with Dance Alive! involved playing the role of Mata Hari, using a script she wrote for a ballet of that title and a performance celebrating the opening of the American Art Wing of the Harn Museum in Gainesville, in which dancers enacted poems about four characters inspired by Cindy Sherman photographs. Among her favorite multimedia pieces was *Swan Song,* directed by Ani Collier and performed at the Hippodrome State Theater with seven dancers, an actor, and a violinist.

Printed in the USA
CPSIA information can be obtained
at www.ICGtesting.com
JSHW082318161023
50289JS00006B/23